Fungi

naturally scottish

Blue corky spine fungus
Hydnellum caeruleum

Acknowledgements:

Authors: Roy Watling and Stephen Ward (SNH)

Author of The Scottish Wild Mushroom Code: Alison Dyke

Series Editor: Lynne Farrell (SNH)

Design and production: SNH Design and Publications

Photographs:

Valerie & Ernest Emmett 29, **Lorne Gill/SNH** front cover, back cover top left, frontspiece 1, contents page, 5, 9, 11, 12, 13 right, 15, 16, 19, 21, 25, 26, 27, 28, 30, 31, 32, **George McCarthy** 1, 14, **RBGE** 6, 18, **Paul Sterry/Nature Photographers Ltd.** 10, 23, **Roy Watling** 2, 7, 8, 13 left, 17, **Chris Watt** 20, back cover top right.

Illustrations:

Jaqueline Stevenson Page 22 **& Kelly Stuart/SNH** Page 4

Scottish Natural Heritage

Design and Publications

Battleby

Redgorton

Perth PH1 3EW

Tel: 01738 444177

Fax: 01738 827411

E-mail: pubs@snh.gov.uk

Web site: http://www.snh.org.uk

Cover photograph:
Pink ballerina or pink meadow-cap · *Hygrocybe calyptriformis*
Back cover photograph:
Scarlet elf cup · *Sarcoscypha coccinea*

Fungi

naturally scottish

by

Roy Watling (British Mycological Society)

and

Stephen Ward (Scottish Natural Heritage)

Foreword

Many of us wouldn't admit it, but when younger, our first action on seeing a group of toadstools in the local park or woodland might have been to kick them over. We did it for no obvious reason, nothing we could justify, even then. It was an act of seemingly wanton destructiveness, rural vandalism. Yet I have always believed that it was something borne of an innate and long inherited superstition, a quite erroneous judgement with a lineage back to ancient times. For centuries, these extraordinary objects that appeared, almost literally overnight, were perceived as abnormal growths, productions of the earth itself, as sinister as they were mysterious. And for reasons that no-one has satisfactorily explained, the British Isles have long been at the forefront of these outdated notions, the epicentre of fungiphobia. This is all a strange and sad irony because, scientifically, we have always been in the vanguard of the study of fungi - the science of mycology. Our mycologists have long been amongst the finest and our national body, the British Mycological Society, is the largest in the world. And within Britain, the forests, fields and mountains of Scotland offer some of the richest habitats for fungi that you will find anywhere.

Only in relatively recent times have those ancient and ill-founded beliefs gradually been replaced by understanding, knowledge and an appreciation of the remarkable organisms that fungi are. But even today, fungi feature inadequately on our school and university syllabuses and are still too often considered to be deviant plants - to which they aren't even remotely related.

So let the wonderful Scottish heritage of wild fungi help put right this wrong. Let your walks and excursions be enlivened by the beauty of form and the colours of the great diversity of the fungi that you will see. Enjoy and admire them, be stimulated to learn a little more about the way they go about their fascinating lives and realise that the mushrooms and toadstools that you see are but the tip of a great biological 'iceberg' below the soil surface, under the bark, on the leaves and everywhere else in the environment. Mushrooms and toadstools are merely the large and obvious reproductive structures of organisms that stretch in almost limitless microscopic growth beyond our sight. Fungi are the great unseen and unappreciated providers of the natural world, assisting the supply of essential nutrients and other chemicals that power life in every environment and every habitat. Be amazed and entranced by some of the greatest marvels that Scottish nature has to offer.

Stefan Buczacki,
Author and Broadcaster,
Former President of the British Mycological Society.

A violaceous fairy club
Clavaria zollingeri

Contents

Collared earthstar
Geastrum triplex

What is special about fungi?

Fungi are the original recyclers. By decomposing dead plants and animals, they provide a sustainable environment not just for nature, but for mankind and his crops. Not only that, if it wasn't for yeast, itself a fungus, we would not have had beer which was of incalculable benefit to early civilizations by sterilising otherwise contaminated water. Nor would we have bread, cakes, biscuits, vegetable cheeses and meat substitutes - all made by the fermenting ability of fungi. Fungi also help in the fight against disease, as the source of some of our most successful antibiotics. They provide food and shelter in the life cycles of many insects and other creatures and, of course, they are used in many of the best restaurants to add flavour to recipes. That fungi are beneficial in so many unseen ways, is too easily overlooked, given their adverse effects in causing some plant and animal diseases and despoiling stored food - a world-wide problem.

One of the largest, heaviest and oldest living things known on earth is a mushroom growing in north west America. It weighs in at 150 metric tonnes, covers 890 hectares and is at least 2,400 years old! Now that's a monster and the same honey fungus *Armillaria ostoyae* is widespread in Scotland!

A honey fungus
Armillaria ostoyae

What are fungi?

Fungi are so different from both plants and animals that they are placed in a kingdom of their own. They lack the ability to make food from sunlight and simple nutrients (a process known as photosynthesis), except in those cases where they unite with an alga to form a lichen. They are a diverse group of organisms, drawn together by a common lifestyle and structure, and are composed of filaments known as hyphae which, bunched together, form a mycelium. This is usually underground or hidden from view in rotting wood. The mycelium produces a spore-bearing body often called a fruiting body which can take the form of a cap, bracket, cup, club, horn, tiny flask or a gelatinous blob. The form with which we are most familiar is the cap shape, as in the Fly Agaric (*Amanita muscaria*), the bright red toadstool with white spots which often appears in the autumn. A few fungi consist of a single-cell only (yeast fungi).

As they cannot make their own food, fungi depend on being able to break down organic matter which, whether of plant or animal origin, living or dead, originally derived its energy from the sun. Fungi absorb nutrients as a liquid resulting from chemical action on the substrate upon which they grow. Once established most fungi have to stay put, but as the mycelium grows, its hyphae are able to colonise new areas and tap into new reserves of food. One group commonly included with the fungi, the slime moulds, act like primitive animals and can actually move towards food.

There is no scientific difference in the meaning of the words 'mushroom' and 'toadstool' and, although modern usage would suggest that a mushroom is edible and a toadstool is not, both terms can be used to describe any fleshy fruiting body with a cap and stem. The Scots term is paddock-stool, paddock or puddock being a Scots word for a frog or toad. Fungus (plural fungi) is a more general term for either just the fruiting structure or the fruiting structure and the mycelium as well. The fungi which grow together at a particular location may be referred to collectively as the mycota.

The familiar mushrooms, toadstools, brackets and elf-cups, collectively known as the larger fungi, are the main subject of this book.

1. Fruit-body connected to underground filaments or mycelium   2. Wedge of cap   3. Magnified part of lower surface of wedge

4. Spores highly magnified beginning to germinate   5. Mycelium produced by spores

How they feed

Fungi are unseen feeders. By breaking down dead organic matter, fungi make it available to growing plants, thereby preventing its accumulation and adding to the overall health and efficiency of the planet.

Saprotrophs

The breakdown by fungi of litter, dead woody material and animal debris releases essential nutrients into the soil. This generally beneficial process can cause problems such as when dry rot attacks structural timbers. Fungi which act in this way are called saprotrophs or decomposers.

Saprotroph - Hairy stereum
Stereum hirsutum

Necrotrophs

Fungi which kill some of their host's cells, be they plant, animal or even fungus are called nectrotrophs. Generally their attack is not fatal. These include rust - and smut fungi, microscopic relatives of mushrooms and toadstools, which need a growing host as they attack new shoots - a life-style known as parasitic. Other fungi cause such extensive destruction that the host dies whereupon the fungus feeds on the corpse. Several larger mushrooms and toadstools fall into this category and are termed necrotrophs. Thankfully there are comparatively few fungi in Scotland which cause disease in man but some of these may prove fatal, especially in patients whose resistance to infection has been lowered in any way.

Necrotroph - Scarlet caterpillar fungus
Cordyceps militaris

Brown roll rim
Paxillus involutus

Biotrophs

Over 80% of our trees, shrubs and wild flowers depend on fungi located either within or upon their roots. In both cases the hyphae scavenge nutrients from the surrounding soil, which in turn they make available to their host plant. In exchange the fungus receives simple organic nutrients and vitamins. In some cases these same hyphae assist the decomposition of litter. Such associations are called mycorrhizas (derived from Greek, meaning 'fungus root') and many of the mushrooms and toadstools we see in the autumn are involved in such processes. Different kinds of mycorrhizas occur in orchids, grasses and heathers. Many mycorrhizas are highly specific and will only be found with particular hosts. Loss of such hosts may therefore affect a whole range of fungi and any conservation management must take account of this.

Some fungi benefit directly from photosynthesis by forming close relationships with algae. This is such a close union that, as recently as the middle of the last century, they were considered to be a single organism in their own right and came to be known as lichens. Whilst the fungi obtain nutrients from the algae, the fungi protect the algae from drying out. This relationship and those in mycorrhizas are termed biotrophic.

Birch roots with mycorrhiza

Just as there are close relationships with plants, there are also close associations between fungi and invertebrate animals. In Scotland, some wood wasps and beetles use fungi to assist them in breaking down food for their larvae. In contrast oyster mushrooms capture eel-worms on special sticky knobs in the mycelium and use their body fluids as food.

How they multiply

Many fungi reproduce by shedding minute spores. These tiny bodies are something like the seeds of a plant, but without the store of food that a seed contains. A single mushroom may shed thousands - in some cases, millions - of spores which are usually dispersed on the wind, by rain or contact with insects and other animals. Other species have evolved more complex methods.

Truffles remain hidden underground but emit an odour which attracts mammals to dig them up and eat them, the spores being liberated in their dung. Truffles are considered a great delicacy; pigs and even dogs have been trained elsewhere in Europe to find them for human consumption.

Stinkhorns, growing erect on the woodland floor, also emit a smell - but of rotting flesh. Attracted by the smell, carrion flies and beetles visit the spore mass. The spores themselves are embedded in mucus which sticks to the bodies of the visitors. As they fly to a new site, the spores dry and fall off and so are widely dispersed.

Some fungi only reproduce by the mycelium, which is hidden within the soil, plant debris or wood, dividing or breaking into two or more parts which are each capable of continuing to grow as separate individuals.

Harts truffle
Elaphomyces granulatus

Common stinkhorn
Phallus impudicus

White stalk puffball - Inchnadamph NNR
Tulostoma niveum

Where they live

World-wide

Fungi have colonised all the major areas of the world: marine to freshwater, lowland to montane, water-logged to desert soils, woodland to grassland.

Scotland's woodlands, grasslands, and other habitats

The larger fungi are generally confined to woodland and grassland communities ranging from lowlands to uplands, including the dwarf willow communities both of coastal dune-slacks and mountains. The white stalk puffball *Tulostoma niveum* is a very rare fungus which is listed in the UK Biodiversity Action Plan. In Britain, it is known only from two Scottish mountains where it grows among mosses on exposed boulders. The only other British stalked puffball *Tulostoma brumale,* is also found in exposed areas but, in contrast, in sand dunes along the east coast of Scotland.

White stalk puffball

Moss beds support specialised communities of fungi. The moss protects the fungus from desiccation and provides insulation which probably encourages fungal growth. Research is now beginning to shed light on the nature of the link between mosses and the larger fungi - especially the elf-cups. Rather than fungi and mosses simply liking to grow together, given the large number of species of both mosses and fungi, there may be very precise links between the different species. Penetration of the host cells of the moss by a fungus may prove to be a common phenomenon. Sphagnum-moss bogs also have their own specialised inhabitants.

Moorland, although generally poor in species numbers, is a promising habitat, especially the higher Scottish heathlands, where a mixture of arctic-alpine fungi may be found. The snowbed amanita, *Amanita nivalis* is associated with dwarf willow, *Salix herbacea* and was described as new to science from the Cairngorms in 1823. It is now known throughout the northern hemisphere, often growing in very exposed sites which are free of heavy snow deposits. It is characteristic of many of Scotland's high mountains.

The snowbed amanita with dwarf willow
Amanita nivalis

A Mycena growing on an old stump
Mycena haematopus

Old grasslands, which have not been treated with mineral fertiliser or slurry, especially those on base-rich soils, support a rich fungal community. Under the UK Biodiversity Action Plan, the brightly coloured waxcap mushrooms (*Hygrocybe* species) and associated fungi found particularly in old pastures have been surveyed. Scotland has been found to be very rich in these pastures.

Unimproved grasslands are characterised not only by waxcaps, but also by a group of mushrooms with pink spores (including *Leptonia* species), several fairy-club fungi and the similar but unrelated earth or snake-tongues. They are often found in large intermixed troops, some growing around the edge of a circle - known as 'fairy rings'.

A fairy ring of cracking clitocybe
Clitocybe rivulosa

Long-established lawns and golf courses, which have received little in the way of artificial fertilisers, may support the pink meadow-cap or pink ballerina *(Hygrocybe calyptriformis)* - a waxcap listed as deserving special attention under the UK Biodiversity Action Plan.

But woodlands are perhaps the most rewarding places to look for fungi as they provide such varied places for them to live. Each species has its own particular niche, be it on old wood, tree roots or simply gaining nutrition from the humus. The more species of trees and other flowering plants present, the more species of fungi are likely to be found. Some fungi are found only on certain parts of that host. For instance some grow only on the leaves, fruit or woody debris of a particular species, while others may be confined to large boughs or the finer twigs.

While plantations of exotic conifers may support a diverse assemblage of fungi, the native, well-established woods of Scotland provide one of the richest fungal habitats in the whole of the British Isles. Several species of the stalked tooth fungi, so called because their spores are borne on tooth-like pegs suspended below the cap, are ancient members of the old wood of Caledon, one of the richest fungal habitats in the British Isles. Under the UK Biodiversity Action Plan many more woodlands have been surveyed for this group of fungi than ever before. This has shown the various stalked tooth fungi (species within the genera *Hydnellum, Phellodon, Sarcodon* and *Bankera*) to be more widely distributed in Scotland than was first thought. In their long-known 'home' territories of Deeside and Speyside most species appear to be doing well. In addition it has been shown that some are able to colonise older Scots pine plantations. Fungal surveys under the Biodiversity Action Plan have brought additional rewards, such as the recent finding of the rare polypore *Boletopsis leucomelaena.* It had been thought that this fungus may have been extinct in Britain; last seen in Speyside in 1963, it was not found again until 2001 on Deeside. Also fungi new to Scotland are still being recorded; including *Phellodon atratus,* a species hitherto known only from North America.

The oak-hazel woodlands of Scotland's Atlantic seaboard also support rare and interesting fungi. These include hazel gloves, a bright orangey-yellow fungus listed under the UK Biodiversity Action Plan and glue fungus. Hazel gloves, as its scientific name *Hypocreopsis rhododendri* implies, was first described growing on rhododendron, but this was in North America on a species of Rhododendron not found in Britain. It is not known to occur on the invasive *Rhododendron ponticum,* introduced from Iberia, but now widespread in Scotland. The glue fungus, *Hymenochaete corrugata,* is so called because it glues dead hazel twigs to living branches in the canopy, thus preventing them from falling to the ground where they would be available to other fungi to decompose.

Hazel gloves
Hypocreopsis rhododendri

Where the hazel gloves grow -
Ballachuan hazel wood, Argyll

Larch slippery jack
Suillus grevillei

Golf courses and parks offer a half-way house between open countryside and towns and cities. Many vulnerable species can be found in these semi-protected areas. Even a city-centre garden has its own fungi which may include species accidentally introduced from garden centres. Little may be known about such species, in some cases even their country of origin. With the fashion for spreading wood-chips as a mulch, several fungi have been found in gardens which would otherwise be restricted to conifer woods. With this change in husbandry, species such as lorels and morels now fruit in gardens in and around Edinburgh.

Paurocotylis pila, a relative of the truffles and a native of New Zealand has been spotted in gardens from the Lothians to Orkney, but how it came to be here is a mystery.

One of our most familiar and frequent mushrooms, larch slippery-Jack, *Suillus grevillei* is not native. It was accidentally introduced to the British Isles with larch in the late nineteenth century.

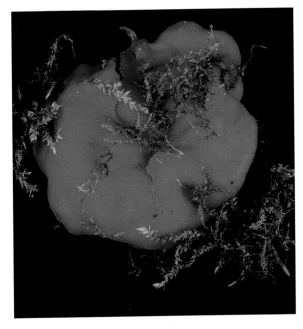

New Zealand truffle
Paurocotylis pila

What we know... and what we don't know

Fungi have been so poorly studied over the years that we still do not know the range of species that occur world-wide; nor do we have an accurate figure for the fungi of the British Isles. Even though Scotland is comparatively well-known, it still holds many undescribed taxa. About 2,500 larger fungi may occur in the British Isles of which perhaps two-thirds are found in Scotland. In addition there are many thousands of microscopic species.

There are already check-lists - nationally agreed reference lists of British cup fungi and lichens. The latest list to be compiled at the Royal Botanic Garden Kew is of the British and Irish higher fungi, known as the *Basidiomycetes*. In contrast many groups of micro-fungi found in Britain are not properly catalogued and we can only guess at their numbers. However, it is indisputable that there are many more fungi in the British Isles than flowering plants - perhaps six times as many.

Crimson wax cap
Hygrocybe punicea

Foraying at Corstorphine Hill

A'foraying we will go

Why collect mushrooms?

As well as collecting fungi to eat, many species can only be named by detailed inspection, supplemented by microscopic examination. Collecting is thus essential for identification. The first step is to determine the spore colour by placing the mushroom on paper or glass and waiting a few hours. Beautiful shapes are formed as the 'rain' of spores reflects the patterns of the gills or pores. As the spores accumulate, their colour can be seen.

Most naturalists begin foraying with the main flush of fruit bodies in August and carry on until mid-October. Several fungi continue to fruit into November or even December, unaffected by frost, and possibly have a second fruiting. Fungi growing on wood may be at their best in winter, even when there have been flurries of snow.

Many fungi start fruiting before August, e.g. May for chanterelles in the Borders. Other species are found only in the spring, e.g. lorel. If one really wishes to get to know more fungi, collecting all year round is necessary.

Fungi and the law

For gourmets and gourmands

In recent years, prompted by cookery programmes and perhaps by travel abroad, where fungi other than the cultivated mushroom are regularly eaten, fungi have become much more popular as food. There are, however, only a few species especially the chanterelle and penny bun - also known as cep, porcini or steinplize - which are chosen as delicacies.

In Scotland their collection for personal use - and by some as a business venture - can sustain limited exploitation. Many fungi are also eaten by wild animals and this is undoubtedly a stimulus to produce further fruit-bodies as replacement structures are ready to spring into growth, provided weather conditions continue to be favourable. Just as picking apples is not regarded as damaging to the tree, picking mushrooms is not generally regarded as a threat to the fungus.

However, expressions of concern by woodland managers about collecting, especially where this is indiscriminate, resulted in a group representing conservation organisations, landowners, mushroom pickers and buyers coming together as the Scottish Wild Mushroom Forum and producing a code of conduct. Trampling is the most damaging factor as, by collapsing the air spaces in the soil and changing water movement, it destroys the mycelium.

Chanterelle
Cantharellus cibarius

The Scottish Wild Mushroom Code

The countryside is a working landscape. Please be aware of safety and follow the countryside and access codes. In accordance with these codes, and as a matter of courtesy, you are advised to ask for permission before you pick mushrooms.

By respecting the natural environment you can help to manage and conserve the countryside. When picking mushrooms for any purpose, please consider the following points:

- wildlife, especially insects, need mushrooms too, so only pick what you will use.
- do not pick mushrooms until the cap has opened out and leave those that are past their best.
- the main part of the mushroom is below the surface, take care not to damage or trample it, and not to disturb its surroundings.
- scatter trimmings discreetly in the same area as the mushrooms came from.
- some mushrooms are poisonous and others rare and should not be picked - only pick what you know and take a field guide with you to identify mushrooms where you find them.

- before you collect mushrooms at a nature reserve please always seek advice from the manager, as special conditions may apply.

If you own or manage land:

- be aware that your management activities may affect mushrooms.

If you wish to run a foray or collect for scientific purposes remember to:

- ensure the safety of your party, obtain permission in writing.
- give a record of what you have found to the landowner or manager and explain the significance of your findings.

This code was created by the Scottish Wild Mushroom Forum, a group consisting of representatives of conservation organisations, landowners, public land-owning bodies, mushroom buyers and mushroom pickers.

The creation of the Forum and the Code was funded by Scottish Natural Heritage, The Millennium Forest for Scotland Trust and Moray, Badenoch and Strathspey Enterprise.

The death cap
Amanita phalloides

Beware

Some fungi are toxic to humans and care must always be taken when collecting them for the kitchen. You might escape with an upset stomach, but - much worse - you could require a kidney transplant or become a fatality.

Three campers near the small town of Lairg, north of Inverness, collected what they thought to be chanterelles, but which in fact were *Cortinarius rubellus* (also known as *speciosissimus*). Sitting down to their meal, little did they know that ten days later the two young men in the party would be suffering from kidney failure brought about by a toxin contained in their misidentified fungi. After a period on kidney machines awaiting a suitable donor, the two underwent surgery. The girl was luckier, female mammals being less affected by this destructive toxin.

Guessing the identification of a fungus is not good enough: you must be absolutely certain.

There are relatively few species known to be deadly, of which small amounts will be damaging to us and other animals. It is not true that animals know better! Dogs sometimes misidentify a fruit-body and are poisoned. Information on poisonous plants and fungi in Britain can be obtained on a CD-ROM available from the Royal

Botanic Gardens, Kew, and the Medical Toxicology Unit, Guy's Hospital Trust, London.

Even those who know the identity of edible fungi should avoid eating fruit-bodies which have been gathered along highways and on industrial sites as their ability to accumulate heavy metals, including radioactive substances, can be high and is a health risk. Always be careful. People who have been at ease eating certain types of mushroom for years can suddenly become allergic. If it is the first time a particular fungus has been eaten, try only a small portion and keep some in case you are unwell; it may be needed for identification.

The rule of thumb is not to eat fungi about which you have the slightest doubt: always consult an expert in the field for a correct identification.

Magic mushrooms

A handful of larger fungi have been used as recreational drugs. Hallucinogenic fungi can be easily misidentified and lead to hospitalisation; over consumption can lead to poisoning. Cultivating and selling fungi for this purpose is a criminal offence.

Conservation

Conserving fungi is not as straight forward as conserving flowering plants. For much of the year the fungi are hidden from view, only becoming visible when they fruit. They may fail to appear for several years, although a fungus which does not fruit may nevertheless be present in the soil. This characteristic, and the difficulties of identifying many fungi - especially in their vegetative state, has made it difficult to build a consistent picture of how they are performing in the field.

New technology is now to hand. Molecular techniques looking at the DNA profile within the soil now make it possible to identify fungi in their vegetative state by comparing their genetic structure with that of known fruiting bodies. So at long last the key role played by fungi in the natural heritage is gradually being deciphered.

At Sourhope Experimental Farm in the Scottish Borders the genetic profiling of waxcap populations and understanding fungal fruiting patterns is under way. The aim is to estimate the diversity of larger fungi species not only as they fruit in the pasture, but also within the soil below the experimental plots following different fertiliser and agricultural chemical regimes.

Cattle grazing on typical waxcap habitat

Dark purple Leptonia growing in grassland
Leptonia nigroviolacea

Caledonian pinewood

Threats

The chief threats facing fungi are habitat loss and pollution:

- habitat loss or change is probably the prime factor in the loss of, or threat to, the majority of our less common fungi. The felling of ancient woodland or veteran trees commonly arouse concern, but how often is thought given to the loss of the dependent fungi? When ancient grasslands are ploughed and reseeded, not only are flowering herbs lost but so are a host of fungi. Even ceasing to graze ancient pasture and mowing it instead may have profound effects on the ability of fungi to survive.

- the term pollution may encompass not only inadvertent air or water borne exhaust gases and leachates, but the increased use of fertiliser to encourage better plant growth has a knock-on effect on their fungi. These adverse impacts can replace a high density of diverse fungi in the soil or on the roots of vasculat plants with just two or three common widespread, and hence successful, 'weedy' species.

Scaly tooth
Sarcodon imbricatus

Woodland management

British woodlands tend to have one major characteristic which sets them aside from woodlands in many other parts of the world. They are frequently neat and tidy, cleared of their fallen trees and woody brash. Leaving fallen trees and dead logs provides a food source for fungi, as well as invertebrates, and is essential if the diversity of an area is to be maintained. Some wood-rotting fungi persist unseen in the canopy or bark of a host tree and quickly fruit when a branch falls to the ground. Other fungi require much longer to colonise before fruiting and several species are found only in very old forests. Indeed the range of wood-rotting fungi is used in Scandinavia as a measure of the suspected age of the woodland.

Aspen fomes
Phellinus tremulae

Red Data List

A provisional list of those British fungi which are considered endangered, vulnerable or rare has been produced. A third of the fungi on the provisional UK Red Data list are species which form a close association with trees.

The Biodiversity Action Plan

Those species for which there is particular concern have been listed in the UK Biodiversity Action Plan (BAP species); over half of these have important populations in Scotland. Whilst the BAP has raised the profile of fungi with biologists as a whole, more significantly it is raising their profile in the public eye. Within Scotland, the BAP is focusing attention on grasslands and their waxcap and earth tongue fungi, woodlands and plantations of native pine with their tooth fungi and oak-hazel woods supporting among others hazel glove fungi and glue fungi.

Earth tongue
Microglossum olivaceum

The Heron Wood Sanctuary & Reserve, Dawyck Botanic Garden

Fungi in nature reserves

Many larger fungi benefit indirectly by growing within nature reserves but at Dawyck Botanic Garden in the Scottish Borders, a nature reserve and interpretive trail has been set up specifically to cater for lower plants including fungi. Here visitors can learn about fungi, their role in nature and their conservation.

Information board

Important Fungus Areas

The fact that the larger fungi only become evident at certain seasons and in certain years has led to their needs being largely overlooked by conservation until the Biodiversity Action Plan began to focus attention upon them. A significant step to address this omission was taken in 2001 when Plantlife, the Wild Plant Conservation Charity, in liaison with the British Mycological Society and the Association of British Fungus Groups published a provisional assessment of Important Fungal Areas in the United Kingdom. Important areas in Scotland cover habitats ranging from moss cushions on limestone boulders to unimproved grasslands and woodland, especially of pine and oak.

Finding out more about fungi

For Beginners

Assinder, S., & Rutter, G. 2003. *How the Mushroom Got its Spots: an Explainers Guide to Fungi* BMS Education Group
Harding, P., Lyon, T & Tomblin, G. 1996. Collins *How to identify: Edible Mushrooms,* Harper Collins.
Moore, David. 2000. *Slayers, Saviours, Servants and Sex: an exposé of Kingdom Fungi.* Springer.
Watling, Roy, Publication due 2003, *Fungi, Life series,* Natural History Museum, London.

Forays

Fungal forays are held annually at Dawyck Botanic Garden, Stobo, near Peebles (01721-760254), and in other parts of Scotland by local Fungus Groups linked with the British Mycological Society and various natural history societies.

Courses

Courses on fungal identification are held annually at Kindrogan, The Scottish Field Studies Association's Field Centre in Perthshire (01250-881286; www.kindrogan.com).

Societies

See www.fungus.org.uk for a general introduction to societies and groups, including links to:

- The British Mycological Society (www.bms.ac.uk) produces leaflets for beginners on collecting and microscopical examination.

Their address is:
Joseph Banks Building, Royal Botanic Gardens, Kew, Richmond, Surrey, TW9 3AB

There are three fungus groups in Scotland:

- South East Scotland Fungus Group
- Grampian Fungus Group
- Fife Fungus Interest Group

The co-ordinator for the local Fungal Groups is Liz Holden (holdens@clara.co.uk)

Field Guides

The difficulties of identification are gradually being eased by the appearance of more reliable field guides.

Recommended field guides include:
Bon, M. 2003. *Collins Wildlife Trust Guide: Mushrooms.* Harper Collins, London.

Courtecuisse, R. 1999. *Collins Wildlife Trust Guide: Mushrooms.* Harper Collins, London.

Laessoe, T. & Conte, Anna del, 1996 *The Mushroom Book,* Dorling Kindersley, London, UK.

Jordan, M. 1995. *The encyclopaedia of fungi of Britain and Europe*, David & Charles, Newton Abbott, Devon, UK.

Phillips, R. 1981 *Mushrooms and other Fungi of Great Britain and Europe*, Pan Books, UK.

Classics
Lange, M. & Hora, F.B. 1963 *Collins Guide to Mushrooms and Toadstools*, Collins

Monographs
Boertmann, D. 1996. *The genus Hygrocybe. Fungi of Northern Europe, Vol 1*. The Danish Mycological Society.

Heilman-Clausen,J., Verbeken, A. & Vesterholt, J. 1998. *The genus Lactarius. Fungi of Northern Europe, Vol 2*. The Danish Mycological Society.

Pegler, D.N., Roberts, P.J. & Spooner, B.M. 1997. *British Chanterelles and Tooth-Fungi*. Royal Botanic Gardens, Kew.

Pegler, D.N., Laessoe, T & Spooner, B.J. 1995. *British Puffballs, Earthstars and Stinkhorns*, Royal Botanic Gardens, Kew.

Pegler, D.N., Spooner, B.J. & Young, T.W.K. 1993. *British Truffles*, Royal Botanic Gardens, Kew.

Scottish Fungus Floras
Dennis, R.W.G. 1986. *Fungi of the Hebrides*, Royal Botanic Gardens, Kew.

Watling, R. 1992. *Fungus Flora of Shetland*, Royal Botanic Garden, Edinburgh.

Watling, R., Eggeling, T. & Turnbull, E. 1998. *Fungus Flora of Orkney*, Royal Botanic Garden, Edinburgh.

Databases and CD-ROM
Royal Botanic Gardens, Kew and Medical Toxicology Unit, Guy's and St.Thomas' Hospital Trust. 2002. *Poisonous Plants and Fungi in Britain and Ireland*.

Also in the Naturally Scottish series...

If you have enjoyed Fungi why not find out more about Scotland's wildlife in our Naturally Scottish series. Each booklet looks at one or more of Scotland's native species. The clear and informative text is illustrated with exceptional photographs by top wildlife photographers, showing the species in their native habitats and illustrating their relationships with man. They also provide information on conservation and the law.

Corncrakes

Secretive, skulking, rasping, loud, tuneless, scarce. . . all these words have been used to describe the corncrake. But once you could have added plentiful and widespread to the list. Now only a few birds visit Scotland each year. This booklet brings you the latest information on the corncrake and reveals this elusive and noisy bird in its grassy home.
ISBN 1 85397 049 2 pbk 40pp £3.95

Red Squirrels

The red squirrel is one Scotland's most endearing mammals. This booklet provides an insight into their ecology and some of the problems facing red squirrels in Scotland today.
Peter Lurz & Mairi Cooper
ISBN 1 85397 298 4 pbk 20pp £3.00

Badgers

With its distinctive black and white striped face and short, squat body, the badger is probably one of the most popular mammals in Britain. Packed with stunning photographs, this publication reveals some amazing facts about the shy, secretive badger.
Mairi Cooper & John Ralston
ISBN 1 85397 254 1 pbk 16pp £3.00

Burnet Moths

Unlike many other species of moth, burnet moths fly by day. They can be easily recognised by their beautiful, glossy black wings with crimson spots. Their striking colouring is a very real warning to predators.
Mark Young
ISBN 1 85397 209 6 pbk 24pp £3.00

Sea Eagles

This magnificent bird, with its wing span of over 2m is the largest bird of prey in Britain. In 1916 they became extinct, but a reintroduction programme began in 1975. This booklet documents the return of this truly majestic eagle. Production subsidised by Anheuser-Busch.
Greg Mudge, Kevin Duffy, Kate Thompson & John Love
ISBN 1 85397 208 8 pbk 16pp £1.50

Seals

All around the coasts of Scotland grey and common seals can be found basking on the rocks, resting between fishing expeditions. Gain an insight into how seals live, their amazing grace and elegance in water contrasted to their clumsiness on land, and where and when you can watch seals in Scotland.
Elizabeth Cruwys and John Baxter
ISBN 1 85397 233 9 pbk 24pp £3.00

Whales, Dolphins & Porpoises

About one-third of the species of whales, dolphins and porpoises known world-wide have been recorded in British waters and 15 species have been found there regularly. Find out how they live, where they can be seen and how they are affected by pollution.
Sandy Kerr (ed.)
ISBN 1 85397 210 X pbk 24pp £3.00

Red Kite

This graceful and distinctive bird was absent from Scotland's skies for more than a century. Now, with the help of a successful programme of re-introduction, it's russet plumage and forked tail can once again be seen in Scotland.
David Minns and Doug Gilbert
ISBN 1 85397 210 X pbk 24pp £3.00

SNH Publications Order Form:
Naturally Scottish Series

Title	Price	Quantity
Badgers	£3.00	....
Burnet Moths	£3.00	....
Corncrakes	£3.95	....
Red Squirrels	£3.00	....
Red Kites	£3.95	....
Sea Eagles	£1.50	....
Seals	£3.00	....
Whales, Dolphins & Porpoises	£3.00	....
Fungi	£4.95	....

Postage and packing: free of charge in the UK, a standard charge of £2.95 will be applied to all orders from the European Union. Elsewhere a standard charge of £5.50 will be applied for postage.

Please complete in BLOCK CAPITALS

Name _____

Address _____

_____

_____

Post Code _____

Type of Credit Card EUROCARD MasterCard ☐   VISA ☐

Name of card holder _____

Card Number

☐☐☐☐ ☐☐☐☐ ☐☐☐☐ ☐☐☐☐

Expiry Date ☐☐ ☐☐

Send order and cheque made payable to Scottish Natural Heritage to:

Scottish Natural Heritage, Design and Publications,
Battleby, Redgorton, Perth PH1 3EW
E-mail: pubs@snh.gov.uk   www.snh.org.uk

We may want to send you details of other SNH publications, please tick the box below if you do not want this. We will not pass your details to anyone else.

I do not wish to receive information on SNH publications ☐

Please add my name to the mailing list for the SNH Magazine ☐

Publications Catalogue ☐